Brazilian Taste Collection
André Boccato & Cooklovers Team

Brigadeiros

Rua dos Italianos, 845 – Bom Retiro
01131-000 São Paulo – SP – Brazil
Tel.: 55 11 3846-5141 - contato@boccato.com.br
www.boccato.com.br - www.cooklovers.com.br

© Editora Boccato / CookLovers

Project Editor: André Boccato

Recipes Research and Development: Henrique Cortat

Editorial Coordination: Maria Aparecida C. Ramos

Recipes Revision: Aline Maria Terassi Leitão

Text Revision: Julie Anne Caldas / Top Texto

Commercial Director: Marcelo Nogueira

Photography: Estúdio Boccato – Cristiano Lopes / Shutterstock

Photography Production: Airton G. Pacheco

The food photography contained in this book is artistic photography and it does not necessarily reproduce the recipes proportion and reality. Those were created and tested by the authors. The effective procedures and results, however, are always the readers' personal interpretation.

Dados Internacionais de Catalogação na Publicação (CIP)
(Câmara Brasileira do Livro, SP, Brasil)

```
Boccato, André
  Brigadeiros: Brazilian Taste Collection /
André Boccato & Equipe Cooklovers ;
[tradução Interchange Idiomas].
  --São Paulo : Boccato, 2012.

  Título original: Atelier de Receitas Brigadeiros.

  1. Doces (Culinária) 2. Receitas I. Equipe
Cooklovers. II. Título. III. Série.
```

12-01177   CDD-641.5

Índices para catálogo sistemático:

1. Receitas : Culinária   641.5

Brazilian Taste Collection
André Boccato & Cooklovers Team

Brigadeiros

A Taste of History	6
Basic Techniques for Preparing Brigadeiro	10
Pumpkin and Spices Brigadeiro	15
Açaí and Granola Brigadeiro	16
Peanut and Cookies Brigadeiro	19
Banana and Brazil Nut Brigadeiro	20
Sweet Potato Brigadeiro	23
Vanilla and Pine Nut Brigadeiro	24
Cashew Nut Brigadeiro	27
Dark Chocolate Brigadeiro	28
White Chocolate Brigadeiro	31
Chocolate with Walnut Brigadeiro	32
Toasted Coconut Brigadeiro	35
Crunchy Coffee Brigadeiro	37
Crunchy Sesame Brigadeiro	39
Different Brigadeiro	40
Tropical Party Brigadeiro	43
Raspberry and Roses Brigadeiro	44
Lemon Brigadeiro	46
Macadamia Nut and Chocolate Bonbon Brigadeiro	49
Passion Fruit Brigadeiro	50
Sweet Corn Brigadeiro	53
Pistachio Brigadeiro	54
Rosé Strawberry Brigadeiro	57
Traditional Brigadeiro	58
Grape Brigadeiro	61
Port Wine Brigadeiro	62

A Taste of History

It's one of Brazilians' favorite sweets, and a must have at party tables.

Regarding its origin, there are many stories, but most probably it was created in the 1930s, in São Paulo. Back then it was hard to get fresh milk and sugar to cook sweets recipes, and with the sweetened condensed milk and chocolate factories in the city, sooner or later they would have found out that if one mixed the two ingredients the result would be a delicious treat.

Firstly it was called negrinho (something like small and black), and this name is still used in Rio Grande do Sul. But during the 1945 Presidential Elections, soon after World War II, some women who were supporting Brigadier Eduardo Gomes (Brigadier is the second highest rank in Brazilian Air Force), who was running for President against Eurico Gaspar Dutra, decided to sell some "negrinhos" as a way to raise money for the campaign. The candidate slogan, "Vote for the Brigadier (Brigadeiro), who is handsome and single" (the sentence rhymes in Brazilian Portuguese), allured the young ladies, who then nicknamed the sweet "Brigadeiro". And the name stuck.

People used to eat the treat the homelike way, the way many people still do in the wee small hours, to satisfy their cravings : with a spoon. The ball shape and the chocolate sprinkles would also have started with Eduardo Gomes's female voters, taking into consideration is was easier to sell per unit.

Today we know that what matters less is the shape and the frosting. What really matters is cooking the mixture up to the right point. The original brigadeiro is made up of three basic ingredients: chocolate (sometimes cocoa powder), sweetened condensed milk and butter -, but we have already developed a wide range of possibilities in the "taste" category. The chocolate itself, formerly the biggest star in the recipe, can be replaced by fruit, grains and even wine to create unusual combinations that can be as successful as the traditional recipe among your guests, and will amaze them as well.

In the next pages you will find a selection of 25 brigadeiros, from the most basic to the most creative, with step-by-step, easy to cook recipes and, of course, delicious!

Basic techniques for preparing Brigadeiro

In a saucepan, mix the sweetened condensed milk and the cocoa powder.

Cook over medium heat, stirring constantly. When it starts boiling, lower the heat and keep stirring until the mixture unsticks from the bottom of the pan and is thick like cream.

With a teaspoon, take small portions of the brigadeiro mixture and roll into small balls.

Roll the brigadeiro in the chocolate sprinkles and place them in small paper cases.

Pumpkin and Spices Brigadeiro

Ingredients

1 cup of chopped pumpkin
1 can of sweetened condensed milk
1 tablespoon of butter
1 teaspoon of powdered cinnamon
½ teaspoon of powdered Jamaican pepper
Shredded coconut to coat

How to Make It:

In a saucepan, cook the pumpkin and smash it, turning it into a purée. In another saucepan, mix the sweetened condensed milk, the pumpkin purée, the butter, the cinnamon and the pepper. Cook over medium heat, stirring constantly until the mixture unsticks from the bottom of the pan and is thick like cream. Allow it to cool down completely. With a teaspoon, take small portions of the mixture and roll into small balls, with your hands greased with butter. Roll the small balls in the shredded coconut and place them in small paper cases.

Serving: 25 units
Preparation + Cooking Time : 1 hour 35 minutes

Açaí and Granola Brigadeiro

Ingredients:

1 can of sweetened condensed milk
½ cup of thawed açaí pulp
1 tablespoon of guaraná syrup
Granola to coat

How to Make It:

In a saucepan, mix the sweetened condensed milk, the açaí and the guaraná syrup. Cook over medium heat, stirring constantly. When it starts boiling, lower the heat and keep stirring until the mixture unsticks from the bottom of the pan and is thick like cream. Pour the brigadeiro into a recipient greased with butter. Allow it to cool down completely. With a teaspoon, take small portions of the mixture and roll into small balls, with your hands greased with butter. Roll the small balls in the granola and place them in small paper cases.

Serving: 25 units
Preparation + Cooking Time : 1 hour 25 minutes

Peanut and Cookies Brigadeiro

Ingredients:

1 can of sweetened condensed milk
2 tablespoons of peanut butter
1 cup of finely chopped cornstarch cookies
Smashed cookies to coat

How to Make It:

In a saucepan, mix the sweetened condensed milk and the peanut butter. Cook over medium heat, stirring constantly until the mixture unsticks from the bottom of the pan and is thick like cream. Remove from heat, add the finely chopped cookies, stir and pour the brigadeiro into a recipient greased with butter. Allow it to cool down completely. With a teaspoon, take small portions of the mixture and roll into small balls, with your hands greased with butter. Roll the small balls in the smashed cookies and place them in small paper cases.

Serving: 25 units
Preparation + Cooking Time : 1 hour 20 minutes

Banana and Brazil Nut Brigadeiro

Ingredients:

1 can of sweetened condensed milk
1 tablespoon of butter
⅓ cup of chopped dried bananas
⅓ cup of coarsely chopped Brazil nuts
Crushed Brazil nuts to coat

How to Make It:

In a saucepan, mix the sweetened condensed milk, the butter and the chopped dried bananas. Cook over medium heat, stirring constantly. When it starts boiling, lower the heat and keep stirring until the mixture unsticks from the bottom of the pan and is thick like cream. Remove from the heat and add the chopped nuts. Stir and pour the brigadeiro into a recipient greased with butter. Allow it to cool down completely. With a teaspoon, take small portions of the mixture and roll into small balls, with your hands greased with butter. Roll the small balls in the crushed nuts and place them in small paper cases.

Serving: 25 units
Preparation + Cooking Time : 1 hour 20 minutes

Sweet Potato Brigadeiro

Ingredients:

250g of sweet potatoes, cooked in water
1 can of sweetened condensed milk
½ cup of sugar
170g of chopped milk chocolate
To coat:
½ cup of cocoa powder
2 tablespoons of sugar

How to Make It:

Drain the sweet potatoes cooked in water and while they're still hot, put them through the vegetable juicer. Put in a saucepan, add the sweetened condensed milk, the sugar and the chocolate and cook over medium heat, stirring constantly until the mixture unsticks from the bottom of the pan. Remove from the heat and pour the brigadeiro into a recipient greased with butter. Allow it to cool down completely. With a teaspoon, take small portions of the mixture and roll into small balls, with your hands greased with butter. Roll the small balls in the cocoa powder mixed with the sugar and place them in small paper cases.

Serving: 30 units
Preparation + Cooking Time : 1 hour 50 minutes

Vanilla and Pine Nut Brigadeiro

Ingredients:

1 can of sweetened condensed milk
1 vanilla bean or 1 teaspoon of vanilla essence
¼ cup of toasted pine nuts
Vanilla sugar to coat

How to Make It:

In a saucepan, mix the
sweetened condensed milk and
the vanilla bean seeds or the essence.
Cook over medium heat, stirring constantly
until the mixture unsticks from the bottom of the
pan and is thick like cream. Remove from the heat,
add the pine nuts and pour the brigadeiro into a recipient
greased with butter. Allow it to cool down completely. With a
teaspoon, take small portions of the mixture and roll into small
balls, with your hands greased with butter. Roll the small balls in
the vanilla sugar and place them in small paper cases.

Serving: 25 units
Preparation + Cooking Time : 1 hour 20 minutes

Cashew Nut Brigadeiro

Ingredients:

1 can of sweetened condensed milk
2 tablespoons of corn syrup
1 tablespoon of butter
⅔ cup of coarsely chopped toasted cashew nuts with no salt
Cashew nut flour to coat

How to Make It:

In a saucepan, mix the sweetened condensed milk, the corn syrup and the butter. Cook over medium heat, stirring constantly. When it starts boiling, lower the heat and keep stirring until the mixture unsticks from the bottom of the pan and is thick like cream. Add the chopped cashew nuts, stir and remove from the heat. Pour the brigadeiro into a recipient greased with butter. Allow it to cool down completely. With a teaspoon, take small portions of the mixture and roll into small balls, with your hands greased with butter. Roll the small balls in the cashew nuts flour and place them in small paper cases.

Serving: 25 units
Preparation + Cooking Time : 1 hour 20 minutes

Dark Chocolate Brigadeiro

Ingredients:

1 can of sweetened condensed milk
⅔ cup of 70% cocoa dark chocolate, chopped
2 tablespoons of cream
Sugar-free cocoa
powder to coat

How to Make It:

In a saucepan, pour the sweetened condensed milk and cook over medium heat, stirring constantly. When it starts boiling, add the dark chocolate and keep stirring in low heat until the mixture unsticks from the bottom of the pan and is thick like cream. Remove from the heat, add the cream, stir and pour the brigadeiro into a recipient greased with butter. Allow it to cool down completely. With a teaspoon, take small portions of the mixture and roll into small balls, with your hands greased with butter. Roll the brigadeiro balls in the cocoa powder and place them in small paper cases.

Serving: 25 units
Preparation + Cooking Time : 1 hour 20 minutes

White Chocolate Brigadeiro

Ingredients:

1 can of sweetened condensed milk
⅔ cups of chopped white chocolate
2 tablespoons of cream
White chocolate chips

How to Make It:

In a saucepan, pour the sweetened condensed milk and cook over medium heat, stirring constantly. When it starts boiling, add the white chocolate. Keep stirring until the mixture unsticks from the bottom of the pan and is thick like cream. Remove from the heat, add the cream, stir and pour the brigadeiro into a recipient greased with butter. Allow it to cool down completely. With a teaspoon, take small portions of the mixture and roll into small balls, with your hands greased with butter. Roll the brigadeiro balls in the white chocolate chips and place them in small paper cases.

Serving: 25 units
Preparation + Cooking Time : 1 hour 20 minutes

Chocolate with Walnuts Brigadeiro

Ingredients:

1 can of sweetened condensed milk
½ cup of chopped dark chocolate
2 tablespoons of cream
½ cup of coarsely chopped walnuts
Crushed walnuts to coat

How to Make It:

In a saucepan, pour the sweetened condensed milk and cook over medium heat, stirring constantly. When it starts boiling, add the dark chocolate. Keep stirring until the mixture unsticks from the bottom of the pan and is thick like cream. Remove from the heat, add the cream, the chopped walnuts and stir. Pour the brigadeiro into a recipient greased with butter. Allow it to cool down completely. With a teaspoon, take small portions of the mixture and roll into small balls, with your hands greased with butter. Roll the brigadeiro balls in the crushed walnuts and place them in small paper cases.

Serving: 25 units
Preparation + Cooking Time: 1 hour 20 minutes

Toasted Coconut Brigadeiro

Ingredients:

1 can of sweetened condensed milk
½ cup of coconut milk
¼ cup of toasted shredded coconut
Coconut to coat

How to Make It:

In a saucepan, mix the sweetened condensed milk, the coconut milk and the toasted coconut. Cook over medium heat, stirring constantly, until the mixture unsticks from the bottom of the pan and is thick like cream. Remove from the heat and pour the brigadeiro into a recipient greased with butter. Allow it to cool down completely. With a teaspoon, take small portions of the mixture and roll into small balls, with your hands greased with butter. Roll the brigadeiro balls in the toasted coconut and place them in small paper cases.

Serving: 25 units
Preparation + Cooking Time : 1 hour 25 minutes

Crunchy Coffee Brigadeiro

Ingredients:

1 can of sweetened condensed milk
⅓ cup of drip coffee
2 tablespoons of cocoa powder
1 tablespoon of butter
Crunchy chocolate balls to coat

How to Make It:

In a saucepan, mix the sweetened condensed milk, the coffee, the chocolate and the butter. Cook over medium heat, stirring constantly, until the mixture unsticks from the bottom of the pan and is thick like cream. Remove from the heat and pour the brigadeiro into a recipient greased with butter. Allow it to cool down completely. With a teaspoon, take small portions of the mixture and roll into small balls, with your hands greased with butter. Roll the brigadeiro balls in the chocolate balls and place them in small paper cases.

Serving: 25 units
Preparation + Cooking Time : 1 hour 25 minutes

Crunchy Sesame Brigadeiro

Ingredients:

⅓ cup of sugar
2 tablespoons of water
¼ cup of white sesame seeds
1 can of sweetened condensed milk
White and black sesame seeds to coat

How to Make It:

In a saucepan, mix the sugar and the water. Cook over low heat and let it boil until it acquires a caramel color. Add the sesame seeds, stir and pour the mixture over a marble plate greased with butter. Allow it to cool down completely and break it into small pieces. In another saucepan, pour the sweetened condensed milk and cook over medium heat, stirring constantly, until it unsticks form the bottom of the pan and is thick like cream. Remove from the heat, add the sesame praline, stir and pour the brigadeiro in a recipient greased with butter. Allow it to cool down completely. With a teaspoon, take small portions of the mixture and roll into small balls, with your hands greased with butter. Roll the brigadeiro balls in the sesame seeds and place them in small paper cases.

Serving: 25 units
Preparation + Cooking Time: 1 hour 35 minutes

Different Brigadeiro

Ingredients:

1 can of sweetened condensed milk
2 tablespoons of cocoa powder
½ cup of coconut milk
1 teaspoon of powdered cinnamon
1 cup of chopped hazelnuts
Colored granulated sugar to coat

How to Make It:

In a saucepan, mix the sweetened condensed milk, the cocoa powder, the coconut milk and the cinnamon. Cook over medium heat, stirring constantly. When it starts boiling, add the hazelnuts. Keep stirring in low heat until the mixture unsticks from the bottom of the pan and is thick like cream. Remove from the heat and pour the brigadeiro into a recipient greased with butter. Allow it to cool down completely. With a teaspoon, take small portions of the mixture and roll into small balls, with your hands greased with butter. Roll the brigadeiro balls in the colored granulated sugar and place them in small paper cases.

Serving: 30 units
Preparation + Cooking Time : 1 hour 20 minutes

Tropical Party Brigadeiro

Ingredients:

½ peeled pineapple, without the hard inner core
½ cup of sugar
1 can of sweetened condensed milk
½ fresh coconut, big and shredded
1 tablespoon of butter
2 eggs
Fine granulated sugar to coat

How to Make It:

Cut the pineapple into small pieces, put the pieces through the food processor or blend them quickly, so as to not liquefy completely. Pour the juice in a saucepan and add the sugar, the sweetened condensed milk, the shredded coconut, the butter and the eggs. Cook over medium heat, stirring occasionally until the mixture unsticks from the bottom of the pan and is thick like cream. Remove from the heat and pour the brigadeiro into a recipient greased with butter. Allow it to cool down completely. With a teaspoon, take small portions of the mixture and roll into small balls, with your hands greased with butter. Roll the brigadeiro balls in the granulated sugar and place them in small paper cases.

Serving: 30 units
Preparation + Cooking Time : 2 hours 10 minutes

Raspberry and Roses Brigadeiro

Ingredients:

1 cup of raspberries
2 teaspoons of rosewater
1 can of sweetened condensed milk
White chocolate sprinkles to coat
Petals of red roses

How to Make It:

In a saucepan, put the raspberries and the rose water. Cook over medium heat, and allow the mixture shrink until it is dense, stirring occasionally. Add the sweetened condensed milk and keep it in the heat, stirring constantly. When it starts boiling, lower the heat and keep stirring until the mixture unsticks from the bottom of the pan and is thick like cream. Remove from the heat and pour the brigadeiro into a recipient greased with butter. Allow it to cool down completely. With a teaspoon, take small portions of the mixture and roll into small balls, with your hands greased with butter. Roll the brigadeiro balls chocolate sprinkles and put them into petals of red roses.

Serving: 25 units
Preparation + Cooking Time : 1 hour 30 minutes

Lemon Brigadeiro

Ingredients:

1 can of sweetened condensed milk
1 tablespoon of honey
1 tablespoon of lemon zests
¼ cup of lemon juice
2 tablespoons of cream
Demerara sugar to coat

How to Make It:

In a saucepan, mix the sweetened condensed milk, the honey, the zests and the juice. Cook over medium heat, stirring constantly until the mixture unsticks from the bottom of the pan and is thick like cream. Remove from the heat, add the cream and pour the brigadeiro into a recipient greased with butter. Allow it to cool down completely. With a teaspoon, take small portions of the mixture and roll into small balls, with your hands greased with butter. Roll the brigadeiro balls in the demerara sugar and place them in small paper cases.

Serving: 25 units
Preparation + Cooking Time : 1 hour 30 minutes

Macadamia Nut and Chocolate Bonbon Brigadeiro

Ingredients:

1 can of sweetened condensed milk
1 tablespoon of butter
1 tablespoon of sugar free cocoa powder
3 tablespoons of chopped macadamia nuts
4 filled chocolate bonbons, chopped
Crushed macadamia nuts to coat

How to Make It:

In a saucepan, put the sweetened condensed milk, the butter and the cocoa powder. When it starts boiling, add the macadamia nuts and cook over medium heat until the mixture unsticks from the bottom of the pan. Add the bonbons, stirring quickly, and remove from the heat. Pour the brigadeiro into a recipient greased with butter. Allow it to cool down completely. With a teaspoon, take small portions of the mixture and roll into small balls, with your hands greased with butter. Roll the brigadeiro balls in the crushed macadamia nuts and place them in small paper cases.

Serving: 30 units
Preparation + Cooking Time : 1 hour 20 minutes

Passion Fruit Brigadeiro

Ingredients:

1 can of sweetened condensed milk
⅓ cup of concentrated passion fruit juice
1 tablespoon of honey
Colored granulated sugar to coat

How to Make It:

In a saucepan, mix the sweetened condensed milk, the passion fruit juice and the honey. Cook over medium heat, stirring constantly until the mixture unsticks from the bottom of the pan and is thick like cream. Remove from the heat and pour the brigadeiro into a recipient greased with butter. Allow it to cool down completely. With a teaspoon, take small portions of the mixture and roll into small balls, with your hands greased with butter. Roll the brigadeiro balls in the colored granulated sugar and place them in small paper cases.

Serving: 25 units
Preparation + Cooking Time : 1 hour 30 minutes

Sweet Corn Brigadeiro

Ingredients:

1 corn cob
¼ cup of milk
1 can of sweetened condensed milk
1 tablespoon of butter
Cornmeal to coat

How to Make It:

In the blender, mix the corn removed from the cob and the milk. Strain the mixture and set aside. In a saucepan, mix the sweetened condensed milk, the strained corn and the butter. Cook over medium heat, stirring constantly until the mixture unsticks from the bottom of the pan and is thick like cream. Remove from the heat and pour the brigadeiro into a recipient greased with butter. Allow it to cool down completely. With a teaspoon, take small portions of the mixture and roll into small balls, with your hands greased with butter. Roll the brigadeiro balls in the cornmeal and place them in small paper cases.

Serving: 25 units
Preparation + Cooking Time : 1 hour 30 minutes

Pistachio Brigadeiro

Ingredients:

1 can of sweetened condensed milk
½ cup of chopped white chocolate
⅔ cup of toasted pistachios without salt, peeled and coarsely chopped
2 tablespoons of cream
Crushed pistachios to coat

How to Make It:

In a saucepan, put the sweetened condensed milk and cook over medium heat, stirring constantly. When it starts boiling, add the white chocolate. Lower the heat and keep stirring until the mixture unsticks from the bottom of the pan and is thick like cream. Remove from the heat, add the cream and the chopped pistachios. Stir and pour the brigadeiro into a recipient greased with butter. Allow it to cool down completely. With a teaspoon, take small portions of the mixture and roll into small balls, with your hands greased with butter. Roll the brigadeiro balls in the crushed pistachios and place them in small paper cases.

Serving: 25 units
Preparation + Cooking Time : 1 hour 20 minutes

Rosé Strawberry Brigadeiro

Ingredients:

1 cup of chopped strawberries
½ cup of rosé wine
2 tablespoons of sugar
1 can of sweetened condensed milk
Icing sugar to sprinkle

How to Make It:

In a saucepan, put the strawberries, the wine and the sugar. Cook over medium heat and allow the mixture to shrink until it is dense, stirring occasionally. Add the sweetened condensed milk and keep cooking, stirring constantly. When it starts boiling, lower the heat and keep stirring until the mixture unsticks from the bottom of the pan and is thick like cream. Remove from the heat and pour the brigadeiro into a recipient greased with butter. Allow it to cool down completely. With a teaspoon, take small portions of the mixture and roll into small balls, with your hands greased with butter. Sprinkle the icing sugar on the small balls with and place them in small paper cases.

Serving: 25 units
Preparation + Cooking Time : 1 hour 30 minutes

Traditional Brigadeiro

Ingredients:

1 can of sweetened condensed milk
4 tablespoons of sugar-free cocoa powder
1 tablespoon of butter
1 tablespoon of honey
Chocolate sprinkles to coat

How to Make It:

In a saucepan, mix the sweetened condensed milk, the cocoa powder, the butter and the honey. Cook over medium heat, stirring constantly until the mixture unsticks from the bottom of the pan and is thick like cream. Remove from the heat and pour the brigadeiro into a recipient greased with butter. Allow it to cool down completely. With a teaspoon, take small portions of the mixture and roll into small balls, with your hands greased with butter. Roll the brigadeiro balls in the chocolate sprinkles and place them in small paper cases.

Serving: 25 units
Preparation + Cooking Time : 1 hour 20 minutes

Grape Brigadeiro

Ingredients:

1 can of sweetened condensed milk
1 tablespoon of butter
½ cup of milk
1 box of powder gelatin (grape)
20 units of Thompson grapes
Sugar to coat

How to Make It:
In a saucepan, put the sweetened condensed milk, the butter, the milk and the powder gelatin. Cook over medium heat, stirring constantly until the mixture unsticks from the bottom of the pan. Remove from the heat and pour the brigadeiro into a recipient greased with butter. Allow it to cool down completely. Wash the grapes and dry them thoroughly. Coat every grape with small portions of the sweet, roll them in the sugar and place them in small paper cases.

Serving: 20 units
Preparation + Cooking Time : 1 hour 30 minutes

Port Wine Brigadeiro

Ingredients:

½ cup of Port wine
1 can of sweetened condensed milk
1 tablespoon of butter
Edible glitter to coat

How to Make It:

In a saucepan, pour the Port wine and cook over medium heat to shrink to a syrup. Remove from the heat, pour in a bowl and set aside. In another saucepan, mix the sweetened condensed milk and the butter. When it starts boiling, lower the heat, add the Port wine syrup and keep stirring until the mixture unsticks from the bottom of the pan and is thick like cream. Remove from the heat and pour the brigadeiro into a recipient greased with butter. Allow it to cool down completely. With a teaspoon, fill small cups with the brigadeiro mixture and sprinkle with the edible glitter.

Serving: 25 units
Preparation + Cooking Time: 1 hour 30 minutes

Rua dos Italianos, 845 – Bom Retiro
01131-000 São Paulo – SP – Brazil
Tel.: 55 11 3846-5141 - contato@boccato.com.br
www.boccato.com.br - www.cooklovers.com.br